THE CHILDREN'S GARDEN BOOK

INSTRUCTIONS · PLANS & STORIES ❦ A VOICE FROM A GENTLE AGE

BY OLIVE PERCIVAL

Decorations by the Author

HUNTINGTON LIBRARY
San Marino, California

CONTENTS

FOREWORD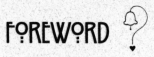

This is a book of suggestions for children to whom destiny has given such golden things as a plot of ground and many hours, or several years, uninterrupted by the city's call (ever more insistent, clamorous) to indoor amusement.

The noises of our world in this Age of Machinery deafen and deaden and too many clever little city children must grow up never knowing the real difference between a house and a home or a public park and a garden.

If, for the first ten or twelve or fourteen years of life, the children of today could have personal flower gardens in which to play, to study, to read, to work, to dream, the world tomorrow would be greatly lightened of its ugly and menacing burden of materialism and general faithlessness.

Because children who grow up in a garden can have no consuming fondness for tinseled melodrama, for life that is lived in over-lighted, mirror-lined places, in the midst of noisy, self-complacent, selfish crowds.

Garden children, no matter what happens to them through the years, find life sweet and big and precious. To them are given vision, poise and eternal youth.

It is easy enough for any child to love a pretty little garden, especially one already made and planted and turned over to him to watch and to care for, at least in part.

In most cases, the surest way to make permanent the interest of the too restless or delicate child is to give him a garden in which the plants and trees, all in their places, are ready to leaf and blossom for him.

Then, day after day and season after season, he will see the loveliness and the needs of favorite flowers and come to an understanding that will result in an enduring friendship with them and all their beauteous, gentle race.

Olive Percival
The Down-hyl Claim
Arroyo Seco

IF YOU EXPECT TO GARDENIZE

If you expect to gardenize and to have flowers grow for you and smile at you (with their roots firm and well covered, all correctly poised on their stems and with their crowns and halos all nicely developed), you will be ever so disappointed unless you really love flowers and love them enough.

Do you know what that means?

It means giving them sunshine enough and shade enough and at the time they need it; and water enough when they are thirsty (sometimes, that will be when you want to swing in the hammock or to read a book or to go for a drive); and protection enough when they are having their winter rest.

This sounds hard. Indeed it is what may be called the supreme test! But in reality it is easy enough, if you like the ever-changing outdoors and want your garden to be a home for all the good and pretty flowers you have chosen.

SOME FLOWERS WILL NOT LIKE YOUR GARDEN

Some flowers will not like your garden and, to prove it, they will disappear. Others will like it so much that they will never leave it, willingly, and they will self-sow and refuse to give up their place to later comers. It is hard to be stern and to dismiss such flowers, even when they are magenta and opaque yellow.

HAPPINESS

Happiness ought not to depend upon applause. If tangible, blue-ribbon success is never yours as a gardener, remember to be grateful for all the wonderful hours you have had in your own little flower-world, watching the wizardry of the sun and the dew-drops and the rain and the mist; all the bird-songs; all the healthful work and happy thoughts; all the air castles and dream-bridges!

LITTLE THOUGHTS FROM GRANDMOTHER'S GARDEN

Long ago, in Elizabethan England and when our colonial history was just beginning, a bouquet was not called a bouquet nor a nosegay nor a bough-pot by those of highest fashion. It was called a tussy-mussy! Nobody seems to know why.

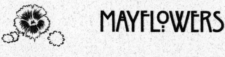

MAYFLOWERS

Once, it was the pretty custom of our foremothers to carry to church or to meeting a small bouquet, or Sabbath-day Posy, the stems hidden in the handkerchief. This nosegay seems often to have been made of sprigs of such sweet and refreshing things as clove pinks or lilacs or cinnamon roses or moss roses or lady's-delight, with the greenery of fennel, dill, caraway, lad's love and bergamot.

It was quite proper to sniff at this and to chew (very sedately) the aromatic seeds during sermon-time, because the sermons were almost as long as our motion-picture matinees of today.

NEWS FROM THE MOSSY GARDEN SEAT

The Hanging Gardens of Babylon were a series of flower-terraces, made in the sixth century, B.C., by King Nebuchadnezzar for his homesick wife, Queen Amytis, daughter of the King of the Medes. These gardens, in the middle of the great city of Babylon, were of such unusual design and beauty (from a distance, they looked like a vast pyramid of green, in midair!) that they were called one of the seven wonders of the world.

THYME BY THE OLD SUN DIAL

Mary Washington's sun dial still marks the sunny hours in a garden in old Fredericksburg, Maryland. It was out in the garden that the Marquis de Lafayette found her, when he went to pay his respects to the mother of his beloved general.

Madam Washington was not expecting him. With a wide-brimmed garden-hat tied on over her white cap, she was raking up autumn leaves and dead weeds, for the pageant of summer flowers was over. It was in the autumn of 1784 and she was 78 years old. The Marquis surprised her but (always a self-possessed small person), Madam Washington promptly dropped her rake and welcomed her caller without embarrassment, leading him to the house and a comfortable chair, where she made him a mint julep and offered him a plate of ginger cookies, listening calmly to all his praises of her distinguished son.

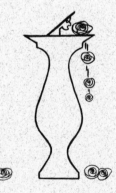

BAY-BERRIES AND BITTER SWEET

The plan for every country place in England and Colonial America once included a plot called My Lady's Garden. In that plot grew the herbs-of-healing; even roses and violets were then classed as herbs with curative values, not merely as pretty flowers. It was then the duty of every self-respecting and helpful housewife to know how to grow herbs (or simples), when to gather them, how to prepare them for use in sickness and how to administer them to the sick and wounded. For, in those days, apothecaries and surgeons and physicians seldom lived in country districts.

ROSE

There is a great deal in a name. A rose would smell as sweet if it had been named skunk-cabbage but, with a name like that, the flower could not have been so well beloved and it would have been left out of much of our poetry.

All of the old flower names have very special meanings and, when we know them all, how wise in old ways we shall be and how eloquently the wayside and garden flowers will talk to us, when we recognize them and address them by all the names to which they are entitled.

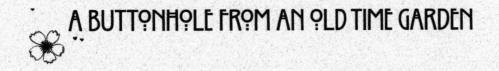

A BUTTONHOLE FROM AN OLD TIME GARDEN

Some morning, write your name lightly and evenly in the soft earth of one of your garden-beds, with a stick or with your finger; and into the letters, quite evenly, drop seeds of cress and mustard. Then press all smooth and flat with a brick. Keep the bed well sprinkled and in a short time you will see wonders!

Is not your own personal name, in your own writing and growing in the garden like a flower, a marvel and a wonder?

Little George Washington thought so when he found his name growing green in the garden, where his father invited him to walk one morning. Your mother will be glad to have you trim the fresh, clean leaves of the cress and mustard, for her tea-table sandwiches.

A PERMANENT CHRISTMAS TREE

A little evergreen, with all its roots and branches on, growing in a pretty box or tub on rollers, can play the part of a real Christmas Tree for several years and then go out to live in your garden. In such a way as this, you become a conserver of our fast disappearing evergreen forests. Every year, as trees are cut into lumber or telephone and telegraph poles, or as they fall in the forest fires (usually caused by careless and stupid campers), you will be saving the life of some beautiful and quite important little tree. Of course you know that countries that do not protect their forests suffer from great droughts and great floods.

WHAT AN AMATEUR GARDENER NEEDS

A Spade
A Hoe
A Rake
A Trowel
A Weeder
A Cutting-knife
A Wheelbarrow or A Cart and
A Basket or two (or three!)

Also, of course, some packets of seeds and a few baby trees and bushes and plants and a watering-pot. I almost forgot the watering-pot and yet I have a new blue one, with bunches of bright flowers painted on the sides! It is strange that the bees have not noticed them.

Of course in the very beginning (and all along the pleasant way until triumph comes), you must have patience, faith. And you ought to have a little make-believe (that is needed now, because everyone seems so practical, so calculating and so nervous, so self-centered!) and a great deal of stick-to-it-iveness.

CATS

Some of the flower names show that cats have a long past as lovers and supervisors of gardens. The observing ancients named many flowers and weeds for them and very appropriately, because all cats do love to stroll daintily along a neat garden-walk, sniffing the leaves and the blossoms, carefully examining all that is new or strange, and then pausing to look fixedly at nothing, before curling themselves up for a cat-nap, in the nicest, safest place in the garden. Being velvet-shod, cats can walk with their four feet all over newly-planted flower-beds and harm them not.

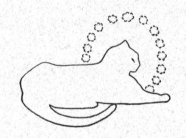

BIRDS

If birds seem to take more than their share of the fruit on your trees, make
a frightener. To make a real frightener, one that will frighten even a blue jay
and a woodpecker, take a large potato and stick stiff turkey-feathers into one
end, for a tail. Then, into each side of the potato, stick feathers to look like
outstretched wings. Tie a stout string around the body and hang this
feathered potato near your fruit trees, in a place where it will catch every
breeze. For, when it sways in the wind, it truly looks like some most
uncouth bird of prey.

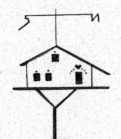

 # A DRINKING-POOL

Please have a drinking-pool of clean water for all the dogs and cats and birds that visit your garden. In hot weather, many nice dogs are thought to be mad when they froth at the mouth from extreme thirst and some quite harmless ailment. A crock or a pan will serve the purpose very well of course, but beautiful and more permanent pools are made of terra cotta and cement and stone and bronze. In my garden, there are numerous pools; three of them are stone mortars, in which long, long ago patient Indian women pounded acorns into meal. In freezing weather, the pool should be filled when necessary with warm water, so that thirsty little birds may not suffer.

OPPOSITE:
Olive Percival's cat on the sundial in her garden

GARDEN PLANS

If I were you, may I say that I would decide first upon the plan for my garden? Without a plan, a flower garden looks too much like a mere flower farm, where flowers are grown only to cut for the market, and not a pleasure garden at all, where it is so entertaining to watch the flowers come and blossom, seed and fade away to rest.

And then I would decide what trees I wanted to grow in it. I would begin with trees and the hedge.

I have sketched some plans for little gardens for you to look at. They may help in the making of a wee, wee garden or of a middle-sized garden or of a great, big garden for any child. Not knowing just how much ground you have, I have not specified width or length. I hope you will like all of the designs and that you will try many of them, as the seasons pass. Perhaps one year you will wish to plant all your ground to bulbs that blossom early enough for Easter and that look like the decorations in your best picture-books, with color-prints by our great artists. (I am not ever going to be too old for picture-books!) And then, the next year, it may be that you will want to plant your garden to chrysanthemums and goldenrod and Michaelmas

 daisies and cosmos, posies that bloom in the early autumn and last until the black frost comes, along about Thanksgiving Day.

Such gardens are very easy and they are fascinating, too. Daisy gardens and cactus gardens are easy. Rose gardens are hard. A midsummer garden full of the many kinds of flowers called old fashioned is thought to be the very hardest. Much depends upon where you live and what kind of garden soil you have to start with. Some people have a very poor opinion of white petunias but never mind! One of the easiest and prettiest gardens of all is planted to petunias, geraniums and daisies, and they almost take care of themselves! These common and very admirable flowers never let you see that they are tired of blooming, month after month, and of keeping themselves neat and attractive. They smile so pleasantly, as you pass them (with scorn or indifference in your eyes), entreating you to love or to tolerate them, in spite of the heartless changes in flower-fashions. How can a flower-lover ever be fashionable enough to dismiss from the garden such brave and eager-to-please flower-friends?

THE LAVENDER WALK

This is one of the easy gardens. The plan explains itself. The garden is planted to Sweet Lavender of different varieties. Some of the little bushes have narrow and some have broad leaves. Some of them flower early and some of them flower late. Some of the blossoms are white, some are dark-blue and some are lavender-blue. A Sweet Lavender garden lasts three years. If you want all the bushes to be nice in shape, the plants should be grown from seeds instead of from cuttings.

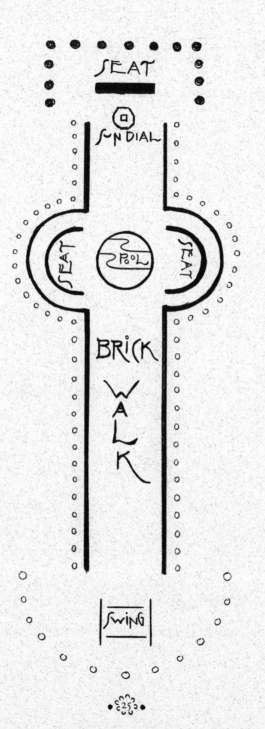

SEAT

SUNDIAL

SEAT   POOL   SEAT

BRICK

WALK

SWING

THE PICTURE FRAME

This is a design for a very simple garden and yet it is one that may be a delight to look at and to play in. The middle of the garden is deeply sanded and the four sides of picture frame are four big flower-beds, held in place by one-inch strips or planks of wood, stained green or gray. In the beds are old-fashioned herbs and flowers.

ALL THIS IS
SAND

THE SLICED CAKE

This is A Pink-and-White Garden. The Cake may be as large as the garden itself, or it may be only a flower-bed, in the middle of a great garden or lawn. Of course each slice of the cake is a flower-bed of pink or white flowers. The narrow paths are graveled. Around The Cake are a Tea Table with Benches, screened by shrubs,

A Tree

A Swing

A Tree

A Bird-pool

A Tree

A See-Saw

A Tree

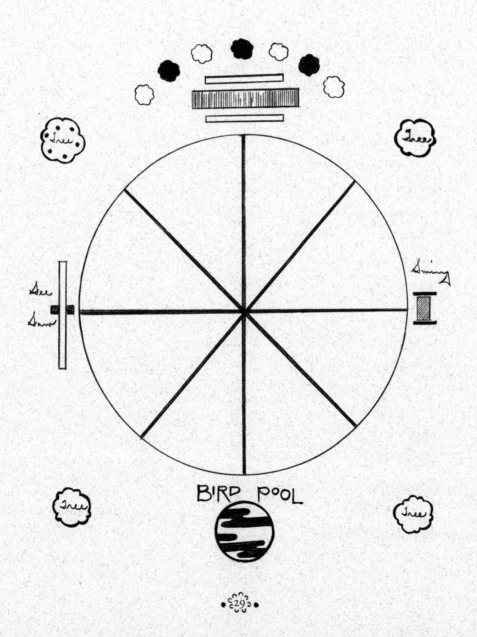

Tree

Tree

Swing

See
Saw

BIRD POOL

Tree

Tree

THE GARDEN OF ALADDIN

This is A Sunken Garden. It is a large garden and one that is hard to make. It is four feet deep, with side-walls of rough stone that are five feet in height, so that they extend above the garden and all around it about one foot and against this rockspray is planted. Stone steps lead down into the garden. Flower-beds are next to the walls, on three sides. A stepping-stone-and-pebbled walk extends down the middle of the garden, between double rows of trees. At the end is a fish pool for coral-colored beauties with fan-tails and for gold-colored ones with velvety black trimmings. This end was a wide walk and a tea table, with benches and also some porcelain garden-seats that came straight from an old garden in Aladdin's own country.

Explanation of diagram:

NO. 1	Seven Dwarf Bamboos	NO. 9	Pomelo Trees
NO. 2	The Magic Stone Step	NO. 10	Persimmon Trees
NO. 3	Flight of Steps down into The Cavern	NO. 11	Strawberry Guava Trees
		NO. 12	Chinese Paper Trees
NO. 4	Walk	NO. 13	Plum Trees
NO. 5	Goldfish Pool	NO. 14	Peach Trees
NO. 6	Table with Seats	NO. 15	Pear Trees
NO. 7	Kumquat Trees	NO. 16	Orange Trees
NO. 8	Mandarin Orange Trees		

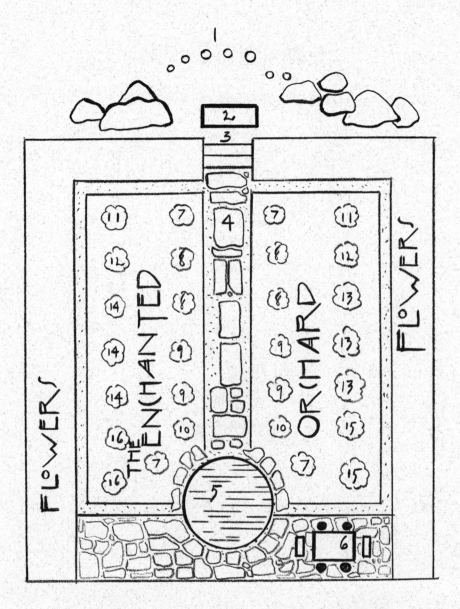

FLOWERS

FLOWERS

FLOWERS

THE ENCHANTED ORCHARD

WILLOW

THE FLYING CARPET

The middle of The Flying Carpet is green, because that is the color of certain enchanting carpets from The Orient. The flower-beds that make the border of the carpet are of bright colors, in diagonal stripes. They are separated by narrow foot-paths, sanded. The center is planted to lippia or sweet clover. All the edgings are quite inconspicuous and, if they are not of narrow, wooden, green strips, they are of smooth sea-pebbles of a uniform size and half-buried in the soil. This is a good plan for a perpetual Pansy Garden.

SAND

PATH PATH PATH PATH

GREEN

PATH PATH

PATH PATH PATH PATH

✳ ✳ PALM~TREES~

THE COTTAGE WINDOW

This is a little garden of eighteen flower-beds, in which you may grow your favorites of all colors. At the top of The Window, there is a Tea Table (with Bench) that is screened by semi-circles of Lilies or Lady Hollyhocks and Snowball Bushes. At the foot of the garden, there is a Pool to dabble in and all surrounded by lippia.

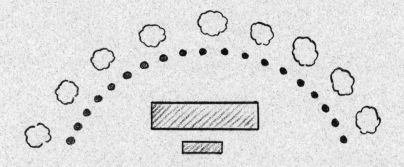

Flowers	Flowers	Flowers		Flowers	Flowers	Flowers
Flowers	Flowers	Flowers	Main Path	Flowers	Flowers	Flowers
Flowers	Flowers	Flowers		Flowers	Flowers	Flowers

Pool

LIPPIA~

THE DESERT GARDEN

Few flowers bloom in this garden. On most deserts, however small and especially in Southern California and Arizona, water is scarce and the dry season is long and glaring. But desert gardens make very good playgrounds. The Hedge enclosing the Trackless Desert in this design is of Indian Figs (Prickly Pear Cactus, with beautiful blossoms and edible fruit) and Variegated Canes (*Arundo donax*).

The Trees by the Palm-thatched Hut are:

    Black Bamboo and Eucalyptus

The Vines are:

    Hop and Tomato.

The Trees surrounding The Oasis are:

    Palm and

    Abyssinian Banana (*Musa enseth*)

The Grasses for The Oasis are:

    Pampas Grass

    (*Gynerium argentium*)

    Zebra Grass (*Eulalia zebrina*)

    Giant Grass

    (*Arundinaria vulgaris*)

    Nile Grass (*Cyperus papyrus*).

Flowers for The Rocks:

    Coral Bells

    Hens-and-Chickens

    Blackberry Lily

    Scarlet Geraniums (Jack London)

    Broom

    Egyptian Yarrow

    (*Achillea aegyptiaca*)

    Jerusalem Sage (*Phlonis fruticosa*)

    Snow-in-Summer

    (*Cerastium tomentosum*)

    Colorado Desert Lily

    (*Hesperocallis undulatum*).

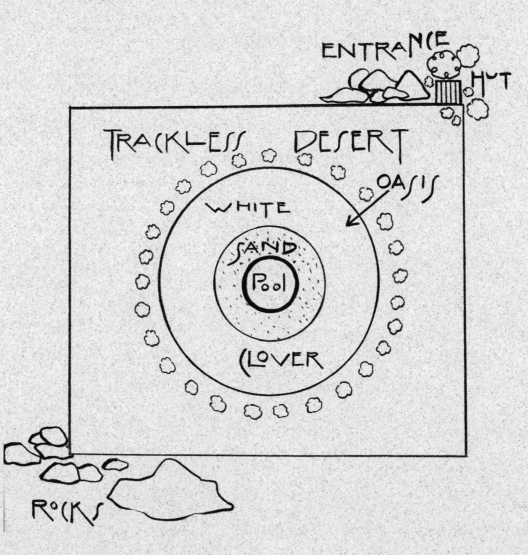

ENTRANCE

HUT

TRACKLESS DESERT

OASIS

WHITE

SAND

Pool

CLOVER

ROCKS

There is a Noon-Mark on one of the
posts of The Hut.
Reliable noon-marks are cut at high
noon on:

April 15th
June 15th
September 1st and
December 24th

THE FAIRY RING

This is A Blue Garden and should have a partially shaded situation. Twelve flower-beds make The Fairy Ring. The center is a green, green grass plot. If one prefers it so (and it would be so pleasant for all the fairies and also it would please the cook!), the center may be planted to lady-mint and fennel and parsley.

Low-growing blue flowers chosen for the segments of the magic circle are:

Forget-me-nots
Vesper Bells and Verbena
Early Borage
Blue-eyed Mary
Blue Butterfly Larkspur
Day-flower
Pansies
Myrtle
Ageratum
Ragged Sailors
Australian Daisies
Lobelia

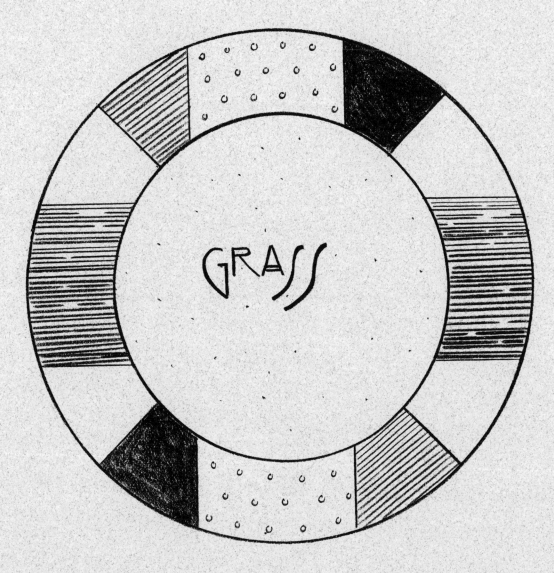

GRASS

# THE KATE GREENAWAY GARDEN

This is a square garden and it is enclosed by a low, green hedge, always neatly clipped. It is planted to grass, in which dandelions and daisies appear every spring. There are two garden gates to swing on, well-built, wooden gates; one is painted turquoise-green and the other red (please use unfading Chinese lead). Two wide flagstone walks lead from the gates into the garden and stop, one in front of a little weeping-willow tree and one in front of an arbored seat, painted amber-yellow or old-gold color. Old-fashioned flowers border the flagstone walks. There is a long, wooden tea table that is painted olive-green. The two wooden benches that go with it are painted red (with Chinese lead). Of course there is a peacock-blue stile, on the far side of the garden. Also there are a moss-green dove-cote and a canary-yellow swing and a turquoise-green see-saw. Between the see-saw and the archery ground, you can see a maypole, painted snow-white! Other attractions in this happy, happy garden are a bird-bath and a permanent Christmas Tree.

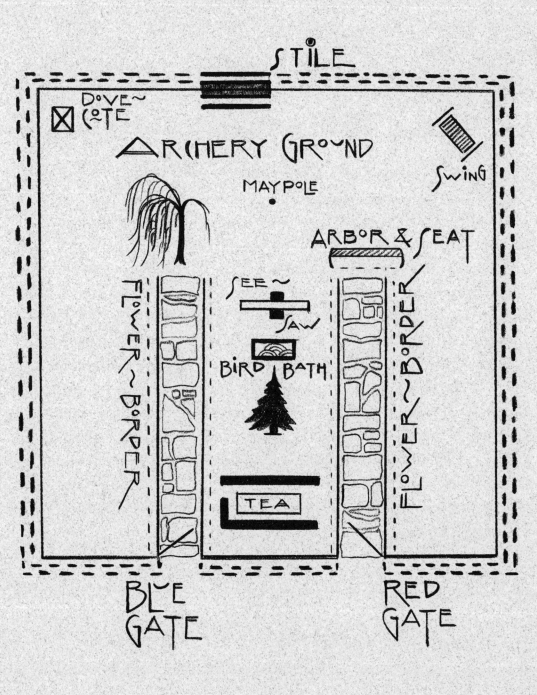

STILE

DOVE~COTE

ARCHERY GROUND

MAYPOLE

SWING

ARBOR & SEAT

FLOWER~BORDER

SEE~SAW

BIRD BATH

FLOWER~BORDER

TEA

BLUE GATE

RED GATE

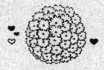 # THE LITTLE THEATER GARDEN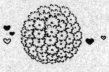

This is a permanent garden. The stage is a grassy terrace, three feet higher than the large grass plot, around which the spectators sit on a very picturesque seat, a semi-circular one with a back, so that no one need fall off backward. It is a very solid seat of stucco on brick. At the back of the stage is a hedge of clipped evergreens or a wall of brick or mossy, ivied stone. There are three entrances, exits. There are two short flights of broad, shallow steps leading down from stage to the flagged walk that separates the stage from the spectators. The great semi-circular seat is screened by bushes of Arbor Vitae or Forsythia or Oregon Barberry or Flowering-Currant or Standard Roses. It is shaded by trees, Italian Cypress and Camphor or Pink Crape Myrtle and White Japanese Flowering-Cherry or Olives or Acacias, with sulphur-colored flowers that look like fringes of wee chenille balls. One ginkgo tree with three Italian cypresses and one Italian stone pine with two camphor trees are given effective places back of the stage wall. Cotoneaster or ferns or hydrangeas grow against the stage terrace. Hundreds of crocuses and English daisies are planted in the grass plot.

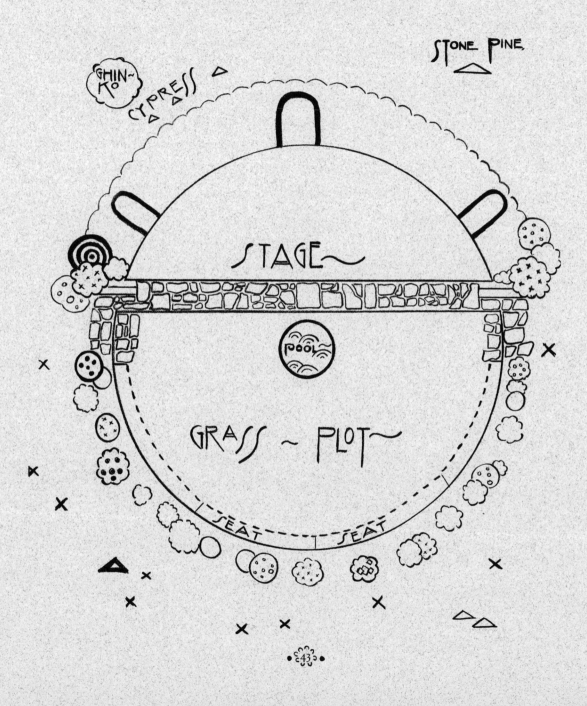

STONE PINE

GHIN-KO

CYPRESS

STAGE~

pool

GRASS ~ PLOT~

SEAT   SEAT

THE MARY-MARY GARDEN

This is, as you can see, a design for a garden that is obliged to be long and narrow. It calls for a graveled path (between the flowers) and such a wide one that any doll being wheeled along its attractive length would easily mistake it for a great boulevard. A Tea Table (or Work Table) is at one end of the wide walk, screened by rhododendrons and oleanders. At the opposite end (all paths you know should lead to something worth walking to) is a Pool for birds or for lilies or for gold-fish. Behind it, in semi-circles, grow Daisy-Bushes (white ones) and behind them some yellow-and-white Four-o'-Clocks and behind them some Hollyhocks of all colors. Correct flowers for the borders are

Canterbury Bells	(white)
Lilies	(in variety)
Pretty Maids	(yellow; violet)
Foxgloves	(white; rose-pink)
Larkspurs	(cobalt blue)
Bearded Tongues	(pink-and-white)
Lady Hollyhocks	(dark red)

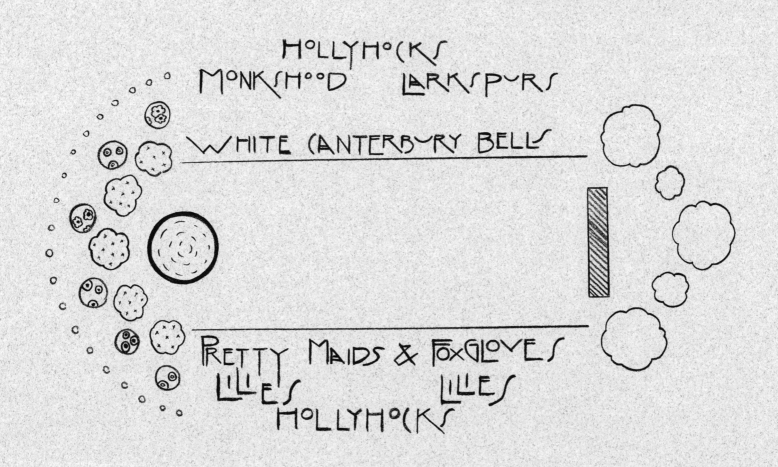

HOLLYHOCKS

MONKSHOOD   LARKSPURS

WHITE CANTERBURY BELLS

PRETTY MAIDS & FOXGLOVES

LILIES   LILIES

HOLLYHOCKS

THE MOONLIGHT PLEASANCE

This is A White Garden and a hard one to make. Two long beds of white flowers are on two sides of the central square. At one end of this grassy plot, there is a shallow mirror-pool and at the other there is a semi-circle of blackly-green evergreen trees, against which are placed seven white terminal statues. Usually, terminals are of the old garden gods or other deities of the Greeks and Romans, but these are quite new ones, being tapering columns of white marble topped by portrait-busts of favorite naturalists, poets and musicians.

Back of the mirror-pool, there is a high-backed seat. A white stepping-stone path through the grassy square and one all along in front of the seat ought to keep the conversation away from the damp and the dew! Two sides of this Pleasance are bounded by lilac bushes and orange trees. Between them and the screen of evergreens are a Magnolia tree and a weeping birch. Back of the evergreen screen are horse chestnuts or gray eucalyptus trees. Behind the great seat are white-flowering shrubs and behind them trees: Pepper trees or deodars or a line of olives.

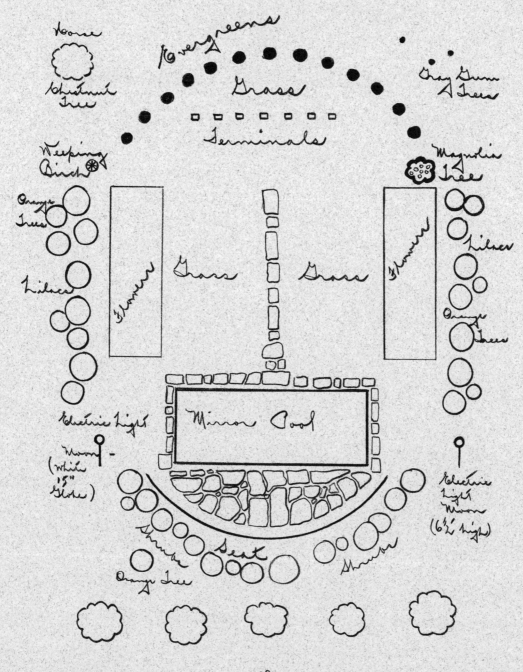

Fcone

Evergreens

Gray Gum Trees

Chestnut Tree

Grass

Terminals

Weeping Birch

Magnolia Tree

Orange Trees

Flowers

Grass   Grass

Flowers

Lilacs

Lilacs

Orange Trees

Electric Light

Mirror Pool

Moon
(White
"5"
Globe)

Electric
Light
Moon
(6½" high)

Shrubs

Seat

Shrubs

Orange Tree

THE POPPY

Between the petals of The Poppy are paths of fine sand. The Four petals (or flower-beds) are planted to

Golden Poppies   Ragged Sailors

Corn Poppies   Blue Flax

Shirley Poppies   African Daisies

Iceland Poppies   Shasta Daisies

In the center is a Pool or a Sundial or a Gazing Globe. Surrounding The Poppy are bushes of Dusty Miller. Opposite the end of each path are two Bushes or a little Tree. Flowers bloom in this small garden from frost to frost!

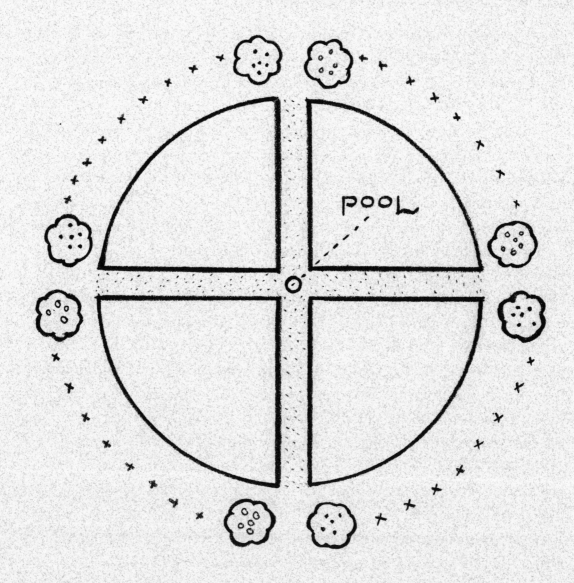

THE REMEMBRANCE GARDEN

This is one of the slowest to grow gardens, because all the trees and shrubs and plants and bulbs and seeds that come to you as remembrancers or that you take home with you, from a journey or from a visit to a friend's garden, cannot be had all at once. But, as the seasons pass, you will think it one of the most entertaining of gardens. It will be much like a favorite book, as everything growing in it will have a well-known story of its own to tell, over and over again. I like a Remembrance Garden to be planted along the sides of a broad walk that is pleasantly shaded by shrubs and trees or that has a fine view over the surrounding country. Then the gardener may take guests slowly along the walk and, if they are interested, explain where all the remembrancers came from.

Often the trees in this kind of a garden are planted by distinguished visitors. In the garden of Mr. George W. Cable, at Northampton, Massachusetts, there is an elm planted by Henry Ward Beecher. The horse chestnut tree in Mr. Cable's garden was planted by Minnie Maddern Fiske. My own Remembrance Garden started with two little trees grown from seed picked up, one perfect April day, from under the great honey locusts at Mount Vernon-on-The-Potomac. Then friends came home from the ends of the earth, bringing such delights as a sprig of lavender from Anne Hathaway's garden at Stratford-on-Avon, a bulb from the classic fields of Paestum and seeds of hollyhocks and marigolds from certain New England gardens, including that of the Quaker poet, John Greenleaf Whittier. And yet, so it must be confessed, the gardener found it hard not to envy an acquaintance who had morning-glories grown from the seed she had gathered on The Great Wall of China!

·❁·

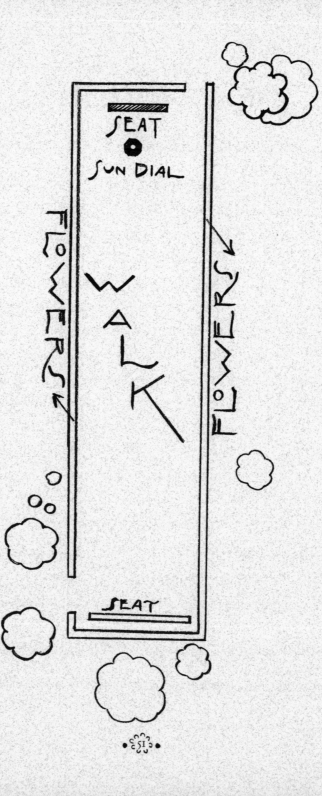

ROSAMOND'S LABYRINTH

❤ · ◎ · ◎ · ◎ · ❤

The Labyrinth should be outlined with box or cypress or laurustinus, clipped once or twice a year. But, if the Labyrinth is to be the garden of A Wanderer, A Mover, and one cannot well wait for the box or cypress or laurustinus to grow up, all may be quite satisfactorily arranged with wire-net fencing (five feet high), tautly stretched from post to post and covered with vines that do not die down in winter. Each post should have two vines and one climbing rose. Here and there, as you grope your way to the heart of the Labyrinth (where of course you will find the Rose-bower), plant little flowers to illumine the gloom—flowers that love the shade—such as yellow pansies, pot marigolds, white sweet alyssum, pink bearded-tongues, daisies, white petunias. Also, there should be several seats. The Rose-bower (where one may study lessons or give tea parties) is an arbor, and it ought to be a pretty tangle of freely-blooming roses. Some of which should be hardy and which have earned the adjective, perpetual! Roses suggested:

Glory of Rosamond (red)
The York and Lancaster (red-and-white)
Red Damask (or Apothecary's) (crimson)
The Black Prince (darkest red)
General Jacqueminot (red)
Bardou Job (crimson)
Seven Sisters (red to rose)

Lady Banks (white or yellow)
Lamarque (white)
Cherokee (white)
Belle of Baltimore (white)
Madam Plantier (white)
Queen of The Prairie (pink)
The One-hundred Leaf (pink)

Peach

Plum

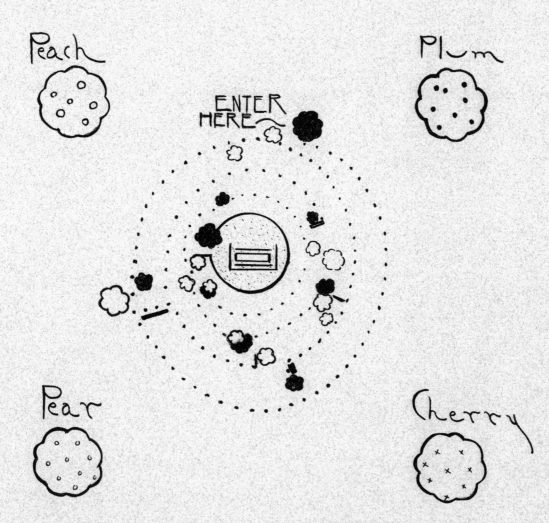

ENTER HERE

Pear

Cherry

Souvenir de la Malmaison (blush)

Dorothy Perkins (pink)

Mademoiselle Cecile Bruner (pink)

Beauty of Glazenwood * (pink to yellow)

Beauty of Lyons (copper-pink)

Reve d' Or (buff)

Glory of Lyons (yellow)

William Allen Richardson (apricot)

*Never prune!

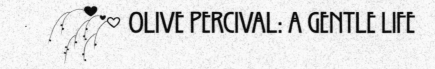

OLIVE PERCIVAL: A GENTLE LIFE

"It is always summer in Los Angeles," a friend told Olive Percival in 1887, "house plants never freeze there, and at Christmas ripe oranges hang on the trees." This was welcome news for eighteen-year-old Olive and her mother, who loved flowers and found their Illinois winters too cold for gardening. As soon as they heard about "the land of sunshine" they boarded a train for Los Angeles and made it their home.

Soon after her arrival, Olive found a job in a department store and began saving her money to build the house of her dreams. At last, in 1899, she and her mother moved into the house that Olive had designed in the style of an old English cottage. She named it the Down-hyl Claim because it was a hilly half-mile walk to the streetcar she rode to and from work. The house had fireplaces but no furnace; oil lamps and candles but no electricity.

The Down-hyl Claim was about five miles from downtown Los Angeles, and it was close to the Arroyo Seco ("dry riverbed"). The Arroyo was dry in the summer, but filled with water after the heavy winter rains. Wildflowers, wild roses, ferns, willow trees, and sycamores grew along the banks of the Arroyo. Artists attracted by the beauty of the Arroyo built their homes nearby. Olive Percival was something of an artist herself. She liked to sketch, to photograph, to make paper cutouts, and to design bookplates and bookmarks for herself and her friends. She also wrote poems, short stories, articles, a book about

OPPOSITE:
Olive's house which she called the Down-hyl Claim

53

Mexico, and a book on old-fashioned flowers. She loved some of the old-fashioned flower names: bachelor's button, prince's feather, touch-me-not, lady-in-the-mist, and never-grow-old.

Little pathways at the Down-hyl Claim led to half-hidden gardens: an old-fashioned garden, a rose garden, an herb garden, a Japanese-style garden. Olive Percival's garden parties were famous. Once she amused her guests by arranging her hats, like flowers, on tall green sticks in the garden. At her Japanese garden parties, cloth koi floated above the flowers, poems fluttered from windbells, and colored lanterns hung in the trees. When the moon was full she would give moon-viewing parties, to look at the moon's reflection in her little pool.

Olive Percival was famous not only for her garden, but also for the beautiful things that she collected. As a saleswoman, and later as an office clerk, she never earned more than $150 a month, and yet she built remarkable collections of books, bookplates, hats, toys, silver, and Japanese and Chinese art. She owned at least 10,000 books, including several hundred written for children. When flood waters from the Arroyo threatened her house in 1914, she filled two baskets with things to save—one basket with her favorite children's books, and the other basket with a mother cat and five kittens.

Olive Percival in her garden, 1915

Olive Percival lived in the Down-hyl Claim for almost fifty years, finding great pleasure in her garden and her books. She died on February 19, 1945, at the age of seventy-five. She once had asked, "What shall endure even for a generation to show that Olive Percival once lived?" She had hoped that a rose might be named for her someday. Several years after her death an Olive Percival Rose was developed, but it did not prove successful. Libraries, however, have carried on her name. There are important Olive Percival Collections at Scripps College, the University of California Los Angeles, and the Huntington Library. At Scripps are her collections of dolls, doll furniture, miniature toys, textiles, hats, costumes, paper cutouts, and valentines. At UCLA are the Olive Percival Collection of Children's Books, her collection of 17th and 18th century literature, and thirty boxes of Olive Percival material, including bookplates, bookmarks, scrapbooks, guest books, and many letters and photographs. Miss Percival's diaries are at the Huntington Library, which also owns more than seven hundred of her photographs, and three unpublished manuscripts. One of them—perhaps her favorite—is "The Children's Garden Book," which she illustrated with dozens of charming pencil drawings. Explaining the mission of her garden book she wrote: "If for the first ten or twelve or fourteen years of life, the children of today could have personal flower gardens in which to play, to study, to read, to work, to dream, the world tomorrow would be greatly lightened of its ugly and menacing burden of materialism and general faithlessness."

Sundial in Olive Percival's garden

Olive Percival wanted her book read by all garden lovers, and especially by young people. It is for these same garden friends that the Huntington has published this little book, with reproductions of Miss Percival's delightful garden plans and a number of her sketches. The book is dedicated, as she intended, to all garden lovers, and especially to young people.

Jane Apostol

OLIVE PERCIVAL'S LETTER TO PROSPECTIVE PUBLISHERS

208 Insurance Exchg Bldg
Los Angeles

To The Publisher
From The Author:

My idea would be to have the book (about 8" x 10") bound in lemon yellow linen; yellow edges; cover lettered in lilac; OR bound in sage green linen; violet edges; cover lettered in green and gold.

The little outline decorations in reproduction-pencil could be omitted altogether, without spoiling the book, although they are the kind children admire, I believe.

The long flower list (to be in small type) helps one identify many of our oldest and once well-loved flowers. The making of this particular list took really years of reading and research (pleasant years!) and I believe the list is the only attempt in our garden literature to give "all" the old folk names, although many garden books give groups of old names in the text (not alphabetically arranged). This feature seems to appeal to all my garden friends here in Southern California.

May I say (explanatively), I have lived nearly all my life in Southern California and have had to teach myself the game of gardening here in this zone, for which no garden books had been written? And it was this experience (and the fact there was no standard garden book for American Children) that led to the writing of this book? And of course the intent was to make a book that would prove of interest and of service both to children and to grown-up amateurs, in ALL zones and climates where gardening is possible.

Many parents and teachers and librarians urged me to write this little book, assuring me that really there is need (among buyers) for such a book,—to start their children thinking about something besides movies and to keep them out of doors.

(Miss Olive Percival)

OLD-FASHIONED FLOWER NAMES

"The names of the flowers are very important and, like keys, open doors to The Great Past, through which we may see many of the peoples and individuals who have helped make this world such a good and pleasant place to live in."—Olive Percival

Here we list a few of the common flower names Olive Percival used in her manuscript along with the Latin names in case the plant experts at your local nursery don't remember the old names.

ACKNOWLEDGMENTS

We are grateful to Jane Apostol, who brought to our attention Olive Percival's charming and near-encyclopedic unpublished manuscript for a children's garden book and then agreed to write Olive's story for this book. David Zeidberg, Director of the Huntington Library, was immediately supportive of a publication. Judy Sahek, Librarian, Dennison Library, generously shared her time to show us some of the charming items in Scripps College's Percival collections. We have enjoyed corresponding with UCLA library student Ingrid Johnson, who, as an intern, helped organize the Percival Collection at the Dennison, and we look forward to her master's thesis on Olive Percival.

As ever, we are grateful to Sharee Wilkerson, our conscientious volunteer who has been waiting for the publication of this book ever since she entered Olive's typewritten text into the computer many years ago.

The photographs on pages 21, 54, 57, and 59 are from the Olive Percival collection in the Photo Archive at the Huntington Library in San Marino, California.

THE CHILDREN'S GARDEN BOOK
by Olive Percival
was set in International Typeface Corporation's Galliard,
an adaptation of Robert Granjon's classical design.
The title and display face is Willow,
a modern font based on lettering popular during the Arts and Crafts period
and reminiscent of decorations in Miss Percival's garden plans.

A first edition of 3,000 was printed by Castle Press,
a company founded in 1931 by Grant Dahlstrom in Pasadena
—near Olive Percival's beloved Down-hyl Claim—
that continues the tradition of fine craftsmanship in bookmaking.
The volume was bound by Roswell Bookbinding.
The text paper is Royal Fiber.

The book was produced
under the supervision of Peggy Park Bernal
and edited by Jean Patterson.
Images from the manuscript were scanned
by the Photo Services Department of the Huntington.
The designer is Lilli Colton.